FROM TINY
BEGINNINGS

FROM TINY BEGINNINGS

James Overholt

Drawings by Iona Overholt

BRETHREN PRESS
Elgin, Illinois

From Tiny Beginnings

BRETHREN PRESS, 1451 Dundee Avenue,
Elgin, IL 60120.

Cover art by Vista III

Library of Congress Cataloging in Publication Data

Overholt, James.
  From tiny beginnings.

  1. Meditations.   I. Title.
BV4832.2.085   1987   242   87-6340
ISBN 0-87178-296-0

Manufactured in the United States of America

Dedicated to our children
John Overholt
and
Beth Bowman

Contents

From Tiny Beginnings 11
Little and Large 14
Created. 17
Evolving 19
Even There 21
That Ye Be Not Judged. 24
The Word. 27
Efficient 31
Redundant 32
Naturally. 33
Halley's Comet 35
Two Trees 37
In God's Image 39
Take My Yoke Upon You 41
Remember Me. 43
Debarkation 44
Do It Yourself 45
All That Was Made 47
Harmony 49
Liking Love. 51
A New Now 53
A Parable 55
Forever 57
A Bad Dream 58

Divine Disappointment 59
Better Than To Receive 61
Brute. 65
Suffering. 63
Confidence 67
Transition. 69

FROM TINY BEGINNINGS

From Tiny Beginnings

Lord, awaken me; I have slept too long. Open
my eyes and let me look as you looked on every-
thing you made. As I walk by the step, and eat by
the bite, and read by the word, so

> Direct my vision to the snowflake
> and the snow-capped mountain . . . .
> Let me see a drop of water
> and the vast oceans . . . .
> Let me look at a candle
> and the sun . . . .
> Show me a grain of soil
> and the Himalayas . . . .

Large from small—
Giant from dwarf—
Enormity from minutiae—
Great love from small cares—
World peace from calm hearts—
Relief of vast sufferings from little concerns.

Awaken me, Lord; let me begin.
My weakness—your omnipotence.
And yet I AM in your IMAGE.
A part of large is tiny.
A part of all is some.

Little and Large

Lord,
　　You have created
　　　　the baby and the adult—
　　　　the sapling and the full tree—
　　　　the minute and the aeon—
　　　　the drop and the flood.

But also, Lord,
　　You have created
　　　　the hummingbird and the ostrich—
　　　　the chipmunk and the dinosaur—
　　　　the grass blade and the sequoia—
　　　　the atom and the solar system.

How revealing, Lord, that not all little must
　　　　become large.
　　If my little is as much as intended, Lord, use it!
　　If my large has become what it should, use it!

Give me confidence to know my own littles
　　　　and larges.

Created

The two were growing side by side:
      the sunflower seven feet tall with a bloom
          nearly twelve inches in diameter, and
      the marigold, barely four inches high with
          a bloom little more than an inch.
      And not far away, a stock of corn, and
          near it a cucumber vine.
Same soil—same sun—same rain—
I loved them all—and every other vegetable and
    flower in my garden.

Lord, I know I do not need to be anything else.
I need only feed on your strength and grace to
    become what you created me to be.

Evolving

There is frequently great effort made to save some bird or animal from extinction. Perhaps this is good—perhaps not.

Who knows what delay in the evoluntionary process might set in? It could be the demise is designed. I am grateful there was no successful "Save the Dinosaur" campaign. Some Tyrannosaurus would have been the end of us all.

As I fancy my own soul's progress along its eternal path, I do not hanker to stay endlessly at some period.

Lord, let my mind be free to expand. Forbid that I should campaign so vigorously for some thought that I keep it overly long. Let it die that a nobler one might come in its place.

Even There

The cathedral at Wies is breathtaking. I gasped
as I stepped inside.

> Ornate almost to gaudy—
> Elegant almost to garish—
> Awesome almost to divine.

My immediate impression was that it took little
effort to worship in that holy place in southern
Germany.

Just as I was recovering my breath, it was
snatched away again as the organist began. Holy
sound added to holy sight lifted my heart to a new
height.

I could only paraphrase the psalm, ". . . if I go
into Wies, Thou art there . . ."

A small Friends Meetinghouse stands in south-
ern Indiana.

> A few benches—
> Some straight chairs—
> Two plain tables—
> A simple cupboard.

The structure is wood frame with plain glass windows. Nothing ornate abides in this building.

It demands the worshiper put his mind on other than material. It insists the important consideration is spiritual. It convinces one to use other than material suggestion to arrive at holy thought. If I go into the Meetinghouse, Thou art there!

Lord, my imagination runs rampant, and I see somewhere in your house of many mansions worshipers from Wies and worshipers from the Meetinghouse exchanging what each has missed and what each has gained:

> Many mansions—
> Many prayers—
> Many types—
> Many styles—
> Many differences—
> Many ideas—
> Many concepts.

Wherever I go, even there will I find Thee.

That Ye Be Not Judged

The rabbit scampered across the garden.
The inchworm hardly scampered, but moved
across a plant or two.
    The inchworm need not cover the distance
    in its lifetime that the rabbit must.

The castor plant grew tall in a single season.
The oak tree barely got out of the ground.
    The castor plant had to get all its life
    lived in a hurry. The oak would have
    years of leisure growing.

One hundred eighty six thousand miles a second
   light eclipses
One thousand feet a second sound.
    Sound satisfies its obligation in
    shorter distances.

Lord, it is apparent we are created to
       move at different speeds,
       mature at divers rates,

pursue varied interests,
attain unlike goals.
The inchworm has its cabbage leaf to cross;
The light its galaxy.
Neither must judge the other.

The Word

"In the beginning was the word . . . ."
I have heard the word now and again!
    The tree leaves wave in the wind,
    The sheep bleats in the field,
    A cloud shifts and adjusts across the sky,
    A baby cries and a mother sings,
    A father tickles and a child laughs,
    A person stumbles and another prays,
        And the word is spoken!
    A congregation sings—a family loves—nurses
        care—farmers plow—children play—
Death occurs—mourners wail—life goes on.

Lord, I have heard it. Let me hear it more. I am
your creation! In all I say and see and hear and
sense, let your word be spoken! "In the beginning
was the word . . . . And the word became flesh . . . ."

Lord, I long for this indelible word:
        Inscribe it on my soul—
        Breathe it in my quiet—

Resound it in my din—
Intone it in my worship—
Proclaim it in my temptation—
Pronounce it in my evil thoughts—
Spell it out as I lie in anguish or rest
in peace.

Let the word be known throughout all being:
Shout the word from the wee dark corners—
Whisper it from the mountain tops—
Skywrite it—
Write it in the sands—
Let the rivers wind out its name—
And the oceans wave to its glory.
Let it fly on thoughts above the life tops—
Let the birds shriek it—
Let the animals bellow it—
Let the sun shine it—
Let the rose exude its fragrance—
Let all flesh exhibit the word full of
grace and truth.

Gracious Lord, in your image
I am part of the word!
Speak me!

Efficient

I walk the country road for joy and pleasure and not for destination. One evening a motorcycle and rider went around me at a tremendous speed. My legs were not nearly as efficient as his wheels. I could see down the road perhaps a quarter of a mile to the crest of a hill. In mere seconds he was over that hill and out of sight. The roaring sound soon followed the sight. I presumed he had some appointment that urged him to such speed.

I prayed the appointment he had to keep was significant enough to compensate for all the joy and pleasure he passed on that road.

My leisurely pace cost me the time, but it saved my day.

Time is never as important as the day!

Redundant

The Pharisee prayed his gratitude that he was not like the Publican. It hardly matters what the Publican prayed; the attitude of the Pharisee is devastating.

Many have been critical of him . . . .

Years later in another society, a drunk fell into the gutter. A passer-by exclaimed, "There, but for the grace of God, go I!"

Many have echoed that prayer of gratitude . . . .

Lord, is there a difference?

Naturally

The weed reaches down into the soil for nutrition. It does not hesitate. It pursues what is natural.

    If the beans and corn can't cope, I must not be angry with the weed which responds in its created manner.

    I like cherries. The robin likes cherries.
    Even though I planted the tree, and nursed it, and sprayed it, and trimmed it, and fed it, I must not be angry with the robin who responds in his created manner.

    I must not be angry with the fox for whatever crimes I may indict him, or the crow, or the mouse, or the poison ivy.

    Lord, I know there are weeds that I must pull, and flies that I must swat. I must kill the beef, the fish, and the tomato so that I might survive.

But let this not destroy my reverence for
 life.
Let me not kill wantonly or angrily. Let me kill
only as it brings higher good into being.

Halley's Comet

That majestic celestial body, Halley's Comet, is a
marvel to behold. It provokes fascinating descrip-
tions in the writings of its observers. So much
about it has been written and read, taught and
studied. Its regular appearance establishes it as
part of the solar system. Scientific enthusiasts wait
through the seventy-seven year interval with
expectancy.

Lord, I would not belittle your comet, but I have
seen sunsets
    far more majestic—
    far more colorful—
    far more visible—
    far more spectacular—
    far more often.

        I think of the full-length sunsets in my life
        that I dismiss casually while waiting in
        anticipation for a concentrated but fleet-
        ing glimpse at some Halley's Comet.

Two Trees

Two trees were cut. From one came the manger. From one came the cross. Who is to say one was greater? Who is to evaluate?

Is the manger greater because life came into being?
Is the cross greater because from here the resurrection?
Or are they inseparable?

Is death so intrinsically a part of life that the two fade into and out of each other?
Is the life pinioned to the manger more lovely because it so harshly promises the apparent physical existence, or
Is the life cradled on the cross more dear because of the gentle promise of existence beyond appearance?
Are the trees of similar stature?
O, You, who created the trees, remind us again of the eternal nature of life.

"Alpha and Omega . . . ." "Before Abraham was, I am . . . ." "For I am with you always . . . ."

And the two trees shall become one tree: ". . . Enter through the gates of the city, and eat the fruit from the Tree of Life."

In God's Image

"It always rains on my picnic."
"I always catch cold on Thanksgiving."
"It's just my luck to have a flat tire."
"Wouldn't you know I'd get the bad one."
"I never win anything."
"It must be nice to have what you have."
"My team always loses."
"It's probably bad news."

Over and over, Lord, I have belittled life, and life is better than belittling.

I know what life must be.
I am your child—
    your creation—
        a part of all you have made—
        and all that you have made is
        ". . . excellent in every way."

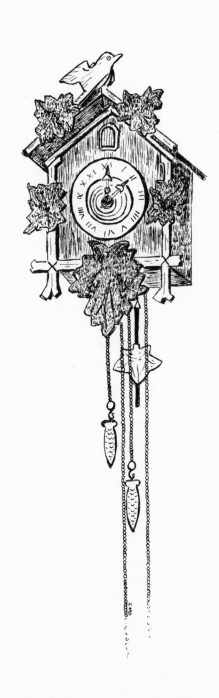

Take My Yoke Upon You

The little bird figure burst from the clock and trumpeted the call of the cuckoo. Twelve times. And the weight attached to the chain below settled slightly with each call. Another weight depended from a similar chain to keep the clock running.

The weights appear huge; but without them the little bird is silenced, the clock stops.

Lord, I sometimes feel the load is intolerable, and yet I know my mechanism is such that soul growth depends on overcoming distress. And distress comes—again and again—as many as twelve times . . . .

Without the burdens, my job has no foundation, my appreciation stops.

Lord, pull the weights back to the top!

Remember Me

Jesus said, "As you do this, remember me!"
I want to be remembered too, Lord.
   But not for my bank account . . .
      or my golf game . . .
      or my television viewing . . .
      or my over-eating . . .
      or my over-drinking.
   Not for the clothes I wear . . .
      or cars I drive . . .
      or deals I close.

I want to be remembered for virtue and worth.
I want them to recall
   Not bad . . .
      But good.
Lord, let me live as though I were dead!

Debarkation

I could hear but not see the plane. The dense fog was blinding beyond a few feet. The pilot's instruments and contact with the voice at the control tower enabled the passenger plane to land safely.

> The landing process is miraculous.
> The instruments are ingenious.
> But they are worthless without the pilot's confidence and trust in them.

Lord, when it is time for my flight to end, I know the landing will be in an unseen and unfamiliar field.

> Give me the confidence and trust of the pilot.
> Increase my awareness that all is well.

Do It Yourself

"Can you play the violin?" asked the man.
"I don't know," replied the lad, "I never tried."

Lord, rescue me from the tyranny of instants. I have been bombarded with instants. Hucksters, advertisers, people with good intentions, people with bad have besieged me with instants:

> Instant paintings—
> Instant puddings—
> Instant clothing—
> Instant furniture—
> Instant organs—
> Instant gardens—
> Instant crocheting—
> Instant composing.

Having seen a Cézanne, a "paint by number" is absurd.

Having heard the captivating theme in Beethoven's Sixth Symphony, a "rendition" on a play by color organ is ludicrous.

That which is fine requires an inordinate dis-
cipline in time, effort, and will.

> I must not belittle my religious pur-
> suit by thinking it's as easy as a tent
> meeting and a sawdust aisle.

All That Was Made

In my reverie
     I fancied I had died and I was in a coun-
seling session with God. We were looking over my
record of performances. I admit I was impressed
with the life work:
     the acts I had done in strength—
     the services I had rendered in
          compassion—
     the words I had spoken in love.

But I was taken aback as God bypassed the acts,
the services, the words, with barely a glance.

     God peered deeper into the contents to
see how aware I was of the
          SOURCE
   of the strength—
   of the compassion—
   of the love.

Harmony

It was a night at the symphony. I can only
marvel at the glorious sound.
> The bow is drawn across the strings of the
> > violin.
> The keys of the piano are played accurately
> > and precisely.
> The strings of the harp are plucked gently.
> The kettledrums are struck—trumpets blown—
> > cellos bowed—flutes fingered—

Each instrument fondled by its master—and
because of the master, from each instrument the
most agreeable tones.
> Nor did any presume to suggest to another
> > how it should sound.

Lord, activate in me that which will release my
> sweetest tone.
> > Let it add to the symphony.

Liking Love

I love pumpkin pie!
 Is it possible I could not like it?
I love a walk down a country road!
I love to work in my garden!
I love to go to the concert!
I love Indiana in the spring!
 Is it possible I could not like these things?

I love my wife!
I love my children!
I love my friends!
I am working to love my enemies!

  I have heard the scholars rant about
  agape and *eros* and *philia.*
I have heard them say I can love without
  liking.
Say, rather,
  I can breathe without inhaling—
  I can eat without swallowing—
  I can walk without moving.

Lord, I live in my own language. I express and
think and do and feel in my own language.
I cannot categorize love.

A New Now

I have experienced
    painful events,
    joyous happenings,
    productive encounters,
    exalting situations.
I am richer for them.

All that has occurred brings me to my present
maturity. I have a wealth in age which is profound.
I have laid up treasures whose value can be known
only in a greater kingdom.

        What a pity it would be to allow all this
        to be petrified in nostalgia.

Experience has prepared me to move forward.
Faith has prepared me to cope with death.
Hope has prepared me to expect goodness.
Love has prepared me to sense the nature of
    eternity.

Lord, forbid that I should overindulge in memory.
With new thoughts to create, let me not
concentrate on a replayed past.

A Parable

The kingdom of heaven is like leaven which a
woman took and hid in three measures of meal, till
it was all leavened.

> One worthy thought encourages another
>   until they are all worthy thoughts.
> One beneficial deed calls another until
>   they are all beneficial deeds.
> Conspicuous joy in giving spreads until
>   all giving is joy.
> Pleasure in sharing grows until sharing
>   offers more pleasure than taking.
> Trust expressed by one widens until trust
>   is common.
> Responsibility assumed by one expands
>   until we are a responsible people.
> One knowing peace influences others
>   until all know peace.

Little measures
of the kingdom swell
until the kingdom is here on earth.

Forever

Line one: "The Lord is my shepherd . . . ."
   Ah, yes, and I can say that without reservation.
   God leads me. God cares for me. I know I am
   God's own. It is so relaxing to lie down in
   green meadows. And so refreshing to drink
   from the still waters. My cup is overflowing.

Line two: "I shall not want . . . ."
   O Lord, I am afraid I must go back to line one.
   I went through it so glibly. I wasn't expecting
   line two. To not want—how can that be? I
   can't begin to list all my wants . . . .

      But you know them better than I!
      And you always have known them!
      You knew them when you wrote line one,
         and you wrote it anyway . . . .
      Lord, you wrote it anyway! You knew!
I shall dwell in your house.
I shall not want.

A Bad Dream

I sat at my table on the busy street. There in front of me were three stacks: one of twenty dollar bills, one of fifty dollar bills, and one of one hundred dollar bills. I intended to give them to anyone who would take them. How surprised I was that most passed by pretending not to notice. It was obvious some crossed the street to avoid me. Some looked the other way. It was hard to believe they ignored me. I had on that table the solution to many of their problems. I thought of the debts many of them had. All could use the money for some good cause. How frustrating to have them pass me by!

Then the strangest thing! At first, suspicious glances—then whispers—then calls—then they began throwing sticks and stones.

Like a hoodlum, I fled in a barrage of shouts and curses . . . .

Lord, how distressed you must have been to be rejected so soundly.

Divine Disappointment

We were just kids—perhaps just a smidgen
more impish than most. His dad smoked Twenty
Grand cigarettes. In those days a kid could buy
cigarettes at Pherp's Restaurant if he told the man
they were for his dad.

> That's what he told him.
> We took the pack out to Pony Creek
> > under the bridge.
> We smoked!

I tried to avoid my mother when I went
home, but she kept getting near me. She said
nothing, but I believe she knew. For quite a while,
I sensed she was hurt.

> Do you want to torture your mother?
> Do something harmful to yourself.
> That is real agony to the one who
> > brought you into being.

O Lord, how oppressive it must be to you when we make of our lives so much less than created to be.

Better Than to Receive

Lord, the idea is perplexing. Sometimes life just doesn't make sense. I wonder if I could be with you without knowing the Christ. Or perhaps could know the Christ without accepting all that he said . . . .

But, Lord, I know!

In those moments when I sense the
presence, I know:
I grow through sorrow,
improve through mourning,
increase through grief.
I rise through falls,
prosper through poverty,
advance through losses.

Let me accept what Jesus showed:
Life comes only when it is released!
Love is ours only when we give it!
Peace is acquired only when it is offered!

It's a hard lesson:
    To have is not to have!
    To get is to give away!
    To gain is to lose!
    To redeem is to release!

He said, "It is more blessed to give."
    That's a statement hard to receive.

Suffering

Our daughter was having surgery. Her mother and I were in the waiting room sharing with each other our gratitude for the doctor, the nurses, and the various personnel involved in the surgery. We felt the care and concern they extended was related to the love Jesus spoke of. Jesus healed, and our daughter was in that process. She would be healed! Jesus healed instantly! That's a miracle! Beth would be healed in four or five weeks. Is that not a miracle!? In eternity, does four or five weeks repudiate a miracle?

Perhaps the pain repudiates the miracle. There would be pain. All on the staff were technically aware of that. But her parents were acutely aware.

> The worst pain is watching a son or
> daughter suffer—
> The worst pain is standing helplessly at

the foot of the bed observing the
    writhing—
The worst pain is suffering vicariously
    with the child.
How quickly the parent would accept
    that pain were the transfer possible.

    Lord, when I saw my beloved child suffer, I
had some vague notion how Jesus could accept
the hurts of the humanity he loved!

Brute

The Hereford stood in the stream drinking.
I stood on the bridge looking down at him.
Something directed his attention to me. He turned his head and stared with expressionless eyes.

But only for a moment. He soon dismissed me and went back to his drinking.

In his abysmal ignorance he was unaware.

Some wiser creature had classified him into species, genus, family, order, class, and phylum. The poor dumb brute sensed only a need for water, and he drank totally possessed of his thirst.

Lord, I stand in the stream drinking. I, too, have been classified.

I have meaning and worth.

I have been created in the divine image.

Quench my thirst. Take me from the stream.

I am more than a poor dumb brute.

Confidence

The supple limb of the willow extended with
the wind. It offered no resistance.
    The night gave way to day without restraint.
    The dew was drawn into the air by the sun.
        The limb, the night, the dew,
        do not presume to know the course
        that should be taken
They have allowed a greater force to be.

Lord, I must be more resilient, and bend or
sway as needs be. I must assume goodness is mine
and will come in a fashion perhaps not clear to me.

Transition

I have seen the caterpillar make its mark on
the earthbound milkweed.
> The worm fares better than the plant.

Remarkably, the milkweed-fed caterpillar
becomes a butterfly. There isn't the slightest
insinuation in appearance or action that the
unattractive larva will transform itself into the
exquisite Lepidoptera.

I have seen a creek wind its way through the
woods and the meadow. I have rested on the bank
and enjoyed its charm. I have studied the water
knowing it would move to the river and then to
the sea.
> It could not stay in the creek.

The caterpillar would not long be a cater-
pillar. If there would be sorrow at its passing,
there would be joy in what it would become.

The creek would always be a creek.
The moving water did not alter that.

Lord, I would rather be a caterpillar than a
creek!